WAITING STILL

God's Glance

MARIE STEVENS

AuthorHouse™
1663 Liberty Drive
Bloomington, IN 47403
www.authorhouse.com
Phone: 1 (800) 839-8640

Published by AuthorHouse   11/20/2017

ISBN: 978-1-5462-0655-2 (sc)
ISBN: 978-1-5462-0656-9 (e)

authorHOUSE®

DEDICATION

This book is dedicated to our God
and the many who could not, have not seen
His appeal and desire for our love not only of He
but all those meant to be
to be loved

INTRODUCTION

Who has seen God? In a smile, a glance, tear or a word? He permits we see, meet and greet Him in our loved ones, family and friends, co-workers, acquaintances and personal interactions throughout the day. A gesture, or kind word freely spoken by another, to the other and at most times when we are not aware. We are loved and are meant to love.

Free to choose love we can nurture the love we have received from our Creator and bless all those He has placed in us, or choose not to concern, deal, treat, ignore others needing our commitment and love. What does it mean? A smile, or word of comfort from our most beloved, friends, family and cherished co-workers, teachers, doctors, lawyers, coaches, store clerks expressing, communicating our natural ability to appreciate, love and respect the other.

This little book is but a gentle glance at some of these small but beautiful relationships we all desire and need to continue on our journey towards God. A God foremost of love, with real desire to connect and be a part of our daily lives. Giving us His greatest gifts of life; others i.e. our own friends, family, acquaintances and even strangers. People to love and appreciate each and every day.

TABLE OF CONTENTS

A New Beginning Am I Worthy?

In the shift of night
Between night and day
I claimed my freedom
And my own name.
May I always seek
And see You
At the dawning
Breaking of day.
Peace and harmony
Are to be sought and claimed
Upon the red of night.
In the morning I trust,
Evening I wait.
Struggles throughout
The dusk of day.
May God permit my name
Be written on His hand,
So that I realize
The dawning
Beginning of a new day.

Amen

What is Most Important?

A word,
Maybe words
Not heard not known
And never seen.
Or a glance,
Slight smile
Deep sigh from within.
Slight stares,
Another glimpse
Remembering a time,
Place not known to any
But only by He,
Who is and will be always.
Ask Him where it is
You are going
And yet, again still
Where it is you have come to be.

Be at peace, always

Amen

THE MANY

For you,
Because there is
A cause amongst
Us all and it is
Called forever.
Forever it is
And will be always,
No matter
Where we are
And with whom
We might be,
Being a people
Without He.
Return then to Him
Enamoured
By you and me,
Though never meant
To flee;
A moment's notice
And then…another
Amongst those
Who never knew,
Never considered
Being in He.
Do you know Him?
Let Him complete each day.

Don't let go!

Amen

NORTH SEA STORM

It was evening and I had just finished the dishes. Claire was making her way over in a bit and I had a little time to put my feet up, relax, pick up a story and melt. Evening was oh so heavy and I was afraid of another out break or storm. Few knew or were aware of the north coast storms, tragedies taking lives during these long winters, seemingly longer still.

So, not wasting any time, I called Claire to suggest we put off meeting for another time when the weather might be more obliging. It was too late. Khris mentioned she had left much earlier keeping her usual habits of errands and occasional visits when having the car. I seriously hoped she would take her time and realize the possible coming of a great and ominous North Sea storm. Both Khris and I were silenced when the warnings and media alerts crossed our screens.

He reached for his home phone, dialed her cell and we heard it ring. How my heart sank! Where was she to be? Do I wait, seek or listen? What to do? As I pondered all, I heard a loud gust as sleet, snow, and ice rang through the back door. Much to my surprise and joy, there stood Claire! Visibly shook and thrilled to have made it on time, she cried tears of bewilderment, love and joy and enjoined us to thank God in prayer.

Amen

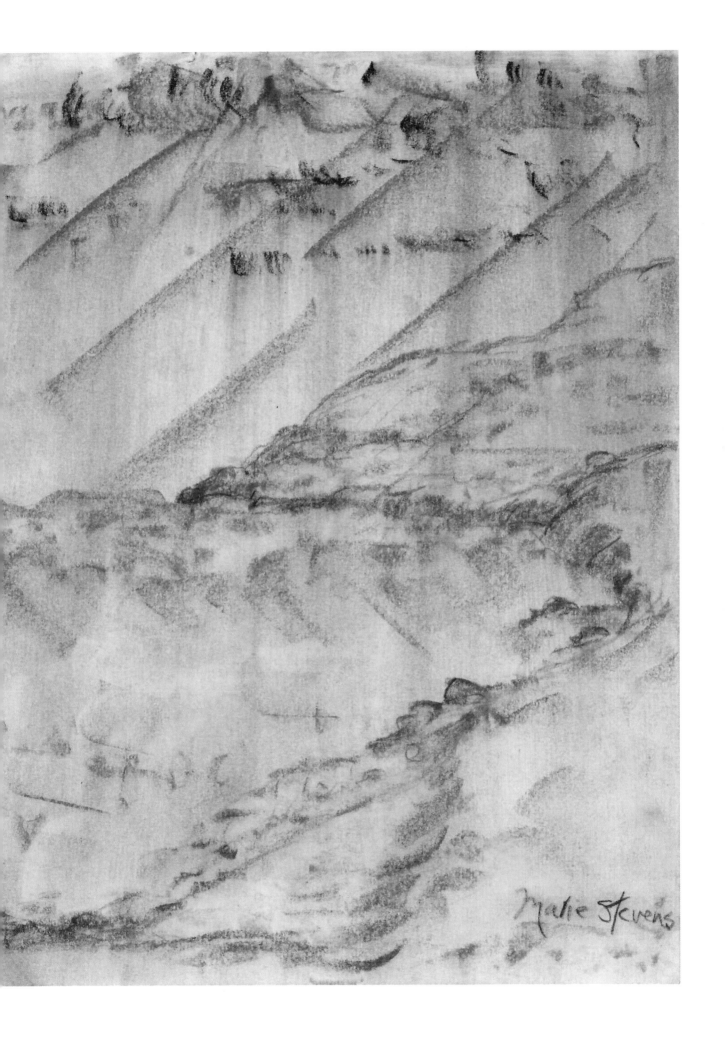

Beautiful

Is all I can say!
Little moments
Thoughts creating
Each day,
Distant appeal now fading
Remember me
Now not seen?
Thought I knew you
One might say,
But no,
Distance came in the way.
A little longer,
and more still
Never to be heard of
Amongst the appeal.
Appeal of the trusted
And many friends too.
Where are you?

Beautiful still.

WHERE HAVE YOU BEEN?

Quiet and subdued
Lasting love and life
From above.
Sorrow of life and love
Below
And beneath
Tears of trouble
Unduly shed
Works unknown to the many
And many more.
Sacrifice
Shedding of sorrow.
New life
Dreams and fulfilment,
Another day dawning.
Sun blissful and full,
Smiling now…
Brilliant gaze upon
Those who remained.
Goodness of heart and soul
And new deeds
To complete the Lord's work.
Another to assist
Each and every day.
Love and laughter,
Peaceful times and greetings.
Accomplishments to achieve
The wishes of the One
Not seen.

WAITING

For you
And within
One more beautiful
And endearing
To each and all.
Loving all,
Placing new life
And graces
For all.
How I have
Waited,
He speak
Mention your name,
Mine too
With and in you.
God's gift and grace
Given us
And all who wait.

Amen

SURGICAL TEAM

Kind word,
Kind words spoken.
New adventures, methods
To achieve what is needed
And desired to treat.
Patients, all kinds
None without need.
Discerning minds,
And hearts
A gentle touch,
Thoughts and words
Throughout the day.
Spirits up, spirits down
Words completed and sundown.
God bless
Your every day
And morning!
Thank-you
Kind words, patience in me

Your patient

DID YOU SEE?

See the light passing
Clearing the grounds,
Rooms and chambers
Properties left behind
And meant to be!
To be created,
Constructed
Formed by He.
In me,
Little works
And wonders,
Wonders of another
Yet unseen,
Unknown by me.
Did you ever wonder…
Who it is who sees?
Sees the candle lit,
Lit only by He.
Change the bearer of light
Light the candle
Let all see!

May it always be,

Amen

UNRELENTING

Clouds of dust and sand burning scratching my skin, hurting scorching my eyes. I can barely see! Where is mother? What was a street busying with people buying, visiting, talking, greeting is now empty and dispersed. Shrieks of turmoil and fear, forlorn is all around.

Mother! I cried but, I knew she was no longer with me. None could hear my desperate appeal for help. Beneath my shirt and short pants the cruel sand etched its carvings and my lungs gasped the air suspended with callous dust and sand. An unrelenting storm invading this tiny outer Calcutta market, only moments earlier safe with beautiful fresh fish, fruit, drinking water, local vegetables, rice, and spices, all for Mom and me.

I struggled to my right, but quickly and away, a gust threw me left, depositing me in a large grouping of old wooden barrels. Protected from all commotion and threat of fierce scorching wind and sand, I was able to see. Peering forward I witnessed a more turbulent menacing storm than I had just come to experience.

I was alone, safe and hidden, from most and all destruction about me. Relieved and thanking God for His help I resumed my search for Mom, no where to be seen. Should I attempt this powerful storm once again, or for fear of injury and possible death, wait let it die down and be?

Hearing a slight rustle and movement behind, I saw a golden saree intricately woven decorated embroidered with red, blue and green. A delicate hand pushing exiting beneath the debris. It was Mom!

"Saakaar" she shouted upon seeing me, "you are safe!"

I reached and held her. Pulling me to her lap and breast, I grasped so tightly as she soothed my trembling aching body with the strength and assurance of her own.

"Never Mother will I leave again. I am sorry for having scrambled away. Be with me, stay with me please."

She kissed my forehead, wiped the dust and dirt from my eyes, hair and face saying

"I'm here. I will never leave."

Amen

Marie Stevens

I'M IN LOVE!

In love
But can't see;
The smile on your face
The glance or question,
Intrigue in your eyes.
The pout and annoyance
Of your mouth when sad.
Can't see,
Always waiting your arrival
No where near me.
Do you know me?
Not really,
My heart beats
But remains still
Still waiting
For you.

I'M SO SORRY

I'm so sorry,
Saw, visited your grief.
Never would have
Wanted it to be.
Had no choice,
For He spoke to me.
Told me:
He loved you
And you were
Meant to be
To be a part
Of He.
Now it is you
Are He
Let it all go
And be.

Amen

I SAW YOU

I saw you
Some time ago
And soon after,
Sweet voice
Words of laughter.
All attending
Hearing
Truths and anecdotes,
Visions and paintings
Song and music too.
Intriguing
Stirring our hearts
To his love joy and laughter.
Words are not enough
But thoughts too,
Appreciation of God's
Gift and word,
Searching, seeking
His love joy and laughter
All in you.

Thank you

Morning Light

Oh! How wonderful is she
Who seeks your face.
Calls coming
Husband allowing
Children seeking.
Worries in the day
But, less and less
Since none struggle
Throughout the day.
Morning light,
Coffees to cheer
Brightening the mood,
And new beginnings this year.
Did you not know
He who is
And providing
Completing this year?
Challenges to be met,
Struggles are kept
Deep within
Defining this year.
Oh, my friend
A dear wife and mother
Committed and
Keeping her cheer.
New beginnings
And love
From the One
Who's face is now
So clear!

God Bless

AWAY

So, it has been
All the while
Since I sought
Your face
Amongst the many
Many strangers
Not of me.
You have placed
Me here
To see, to be
Years now in between.
Where is my place?
Home amongst these…
Not known since a while.
Look a smile,
A tear
Some joy and cheer
From the One
Bringing us near.
Near to these
With hopes and wishes
Most clear.
Teach us, keep us
Place us with you
Now and always.
Father, help us to achieve
Your place today
Tomorrow
And throughout
The years.
Help me Father
Is it here?

Live with us,

Amen

I LOVED YOU!

I loved you
Then and now
But time, place and space
Got in our way.
Another day
Life leaving
Creating another trace
Far away.
Never saw you again,
Saw, heard you were happy
And on the mend.
New life,
New works and words
Another capable
And happy
Worthy of your
Grace and integrity
Laughter
Throughout the years.

Thank you

MID CONGO

Sun was rising and the smell of night passing. My child and I huddled together in our hut upon the worn mat given me by my aunt. My son, my reason, desire to continue still resting, sleeping in my arms. Our hut has tears and leaks but, okay for Geoffroy and me. In the past it was used for storage of grains during high seasons, but there are no more.

My husband Armand, my father's brother took me young and I had Geoffroy. I am the least seen amongst the relatives and dwell with my child at the end of the row. All good for me, I am able to care for my son.

I have not seen, nor been visited by my husband, now away since several days, trading and bringing back all we need. They ignore me you know due to my youth and infant child. The other wives older, children too, enjoy my husband's favour and status. Some able to join him on excursions to help bring back food and supplies. We are the last to receive. All well, Geoffroy is cared for and happy.

I will rise, take the jugs and travel for water so that all can start their day. It worries me to leave him so young but it must be done. Nothing to eat since several days and my son is growing weak, he will need to eat. I will while dropping water at my husband's house see if there is any food for Geoffroy and me.

Mid day sun beating down I see the village and our stream of houses curving, mounting the hill. My family must be thirsty and maybe my husband has returned. I leave the jugs and am given a plate of rations for the day.

Returning to my place I do not see Geoffroy. He is missing. A cull on a lioness has recently been called. She wanders too close to the village. Small children have disappeared. Where are you my son? Mommy is home and lots to eat, water to drink. I am home, Mom's here!

He did not answer and was not to be seen, so I returned to the main house. No one has seen Geoffroy, barely three, thought he was just with the others, about in the streets. God, I plead bring Geoffroy to me, make him safe, Mom's home finally, come and see!

I searched, we searched for Geoffroy but, he was no where to be found. As the days and weeks passed I cried God bring him to me. Silence, deep loneliness gripped my nights, mourning and despair my days.

Over time, with Geoffroy safeguarding keeping my dreams another child moved within me. I lamented, prayed God keep him, place him, now and always with me. Let him be the smile of my days, the comfort of my nights, the joy, love, honour of his big brother Geoffroy and me.

Amen

FATHER

Who is it who can say
I never knew you?
I never knew
Your kind and gentle way.
The measure of steps
Taken in your day.
Living life to the fullest,
Although
Many empty moments existed
Along the way.
Fish, clean, be proper
For another journeyed day.
See the sun
Melt into the night,
And rise
To another eventful day
Soul of love
And laughter, dance.
Joy deep down
Guiding the way.
Seek the One
And only One
Who knows your every day.
God bless the man
Who never lost his way.
Love, peace, and tranquility
Await you,
Now and always.

Amen

DAUGHTER

No one has forgotten you!
For the least not He.
He who reigns,
Who is
And always
Will be.
Achieve Him
Who loves you
More and more than ever.
There is only one
Who will speak
Goodness and kindness,
Laughter and love
From above.
Seek His ways
And wishes too,
For he is
and always in you!
You shall never regret,
Nor ever forget,
Nor be forgotten
By He.
Grab a box
Wrap Him within
Keep Him with you
And within.

Amen

MOM

Considered way,
Considering all in need.
Helpful, truly lovely,
A part of those in need.
Giving, giving hands
Small and tidy, strong of grasp.
Little jokes, smiles and greetings
Diners and dishes done and placed.
Times of rejoicing, jokes and laughter
Upon their face.
Appreciation of the one
Giving and given
To all those in need.

Amen

SON

Seeking eyes,
Soul and spirit.
Open face,
Rich and beautiful smile
Handsome blond, brown eyed
Youth and child.
How long have I known you?
Not enough;
No one can appreciate
Your truthfulness, strength,
Goodness and determination,
All spent on those you love
Meet and greet
Throughout your day.
Mystique exists in you
Strength and concern
For your own
Lives in you.
Remember me,
A little prayer
In times of need.
A need to be loved
Mostly by He.
A whisper, a sigh,
Thought or a glance,
All created by He!
Seek Him therefore,
In silent moments
Known only by He.
May you always
Be loved and blessed!

Amen

Dubai Central

Oh, what a hub of colour and beauty! Dad has placed me here a few days to see what I think, get a feel for the next annual meeting. Very nice! This is one of the most luxurious hotels and the amenities are great. Everyone will certainly enjoy this space. So much to see! I'll have to grasp an overview, what people may enjoy during their down time and just print it out, display all for upcoming attendees.

Mom, she's on my mind lately, her health is not great. Seems to need more rest than usual. I'll check in after scouting the premises.

Wow! Look at this balcony great views from all around. Truly spectacular, buildings so immense, properties expansive and exquisite, all for the viewing and visiting and then some. Imagine the parties and late nights! For now, I'll get acquainted, look and see, experience more later.

"Mr. Lesley" as a knock comes to my door, "have an urgent message for you. Your Father has been trying to connect with you."

Oh, haven't thought to check my messages, been caught up in seeing all. Funny can't find my cell phone. I'll look later.

"Yes sir, what do you have for me?"

"Your Father wants you to call right away if possible?"

"Certainly thanks!"

"Ya, Dad what's up?"

"Well your mother has taken a turn for the worst and an ambulance has taken her to hospital. I will be joining her shortly, so I need you to take over in Dubai. I'll be in touch. Talk soon."

This worries me. I knew Mom wasn't herself. Well then, where to start? I'll get hold of some divisional managers and we'll go from there.

"Jack can you reach Heather and contact me through my room number 3517, I've misplaced my cell phone. There has been a major change."

Now that I left a message I'll check with front desk, maybe someone has seen my cell phone.

"Yes Sir, Dubai Limousine has just dropped a cell phone, we assume it may be yours? We'll run that up immediately."

Good! Now I can get started, but I'll check home first. No answer, I'll text. Alright, back to the matters at hand.

"Hi Jack, were you able to get a hold of Heather? Meet me in my room please as soon as you can." Oh, a text from Dad.

"David leave all with Jack and Heather. Mom and I need you now."

Arriving at Kennedy Airport, the day was overcast. Cold and drizzle permeated the air. Mom is everything to me. I love Dad, but Mom says little gives much, all her love. I am spoiled, her only son.

Dad's copter awaited me and Dad too. We met on the tarmac and I embraced his shaking body. His grief was overwhelming!

"Oh God!" I cried. My entire worth and world came tumbling down. I fell to my knees, was cold and numb. Heard nothing else but Mom's faint whisper, the stare of her kind blue eyes, smile, kiss upon my face and her loving recital;

"Remember David thank and bless your Lord every day, your Father too loves you and has given you much. We are truly blessed and protected, guarded beneath His wing. He shall never leave, love and be with you always."

My hands outstretched, face inches from the pavement, I implored my Lord; please keep her with us, with me! Don't permit she leave. Teach us her joy and laughter, songs of love now and always. Don't leave us. Guide, protect and keep us true to she and You.

Amen

Marie Stevens

UNREQUITED

Seeing you
Searching words to say.
No words can
Replace your gaze.
A blink,
Slight smile
Is all I can hope to see.
When will you notice
Witness,
It is only
You I seek!
And so, another day
Time far away.
Hearing you,
Hope embraces my day.
When will you
Turn, notice my gaze?
Searching
Seeking still,
Where have you gone?
Without a trace...
Little to lead me
Your way.

Amen

DISAPPOINTED

Once again
You have taken
Your life and
Love elsewhere
To be
Not in me.
Again,
You have chosen
Another not me.
How long must
I wait?
Not my choice
But He,
More beautiful
Knowing, loving
Believing, trusting
Of your eventual
Being in He.
I am sorry
He has committed
Me to remain
Once again.
See Him,
Look to Him

Trust and thank Him,
For His love is forever
And always lasting.
Disappointed
And desiring
Hopeful
On freeing soon,
I wait.
What love is it
Now and always
Must wait,
Never be
Due to one seeking
Being elsewhere
Not in me?
May God forgive
My lack of trust In He.
I love Him,
And now you too.
Please see me.

When will I be free?

Amen

SORROW

Sorrow in a glance.
Have you seen my sorrow?
Hidden for now,
All beneath
Beyond what is seen.
Seen possibly in a glance,
Revealed, unprotected
In your eyes.
Eyes lovely,
Knowing of me.
Would you stay
Witness my sorrow?
Gone now,
With you here
And part of me.
Take my hand,
Let me see;
Are you here
To assist and guide me?
Lord, I have
Reached for you
And you have
Witnessed my sorrow.
Please
Return your joy to me.
Stay with me.
I trust in you!

Amen

PROLOGUE

It is in the quiet and still and unseen we might listen, wait and greet our God. His presence is throughout and sensed when we are happy, sad, alone or amongst the many. He is and will always be our hope and inspiration, great desire and love, endless and eternal. Many do not know Him, or, quite simply have forgotten Him, but that does not make Him any less, not He, only you and me.

This little book touches not only our own selves and ability to love but the love of God Himself. May we always request and be assured of His great presence, love and attraction to all His people. Speak to Him you will see Him standing before you attending to your requests, needs, hopes and desires. He loves you.

In a sequel to this book I will continue to explore love; the love of God and of you and me. He is and always will be our greatest love.

Amen